EPIPHANY

A COLLECTION

Sarah Allen

Presentation by *BookLeaf Publishing*

Web: www.bookleafpub.com

E-mail: info@bookleafpub.com

ISBN: 9789358360042

First edition 2021

ACKNOWLEDGEMENTS

Thank you to my incredible family and friends for motivating me every day to write more and write better. You are my everything. Thank you Momma for continually teaching me that my art matters, that my voice matters. Very few people (three, I think) really knew about this collection while it was in progress, but those who did were absolutely instrumental in its completion. Thank you to Willow for all the midnight FaceTime calls, the check-ins, and for being my ever-present inspiration; I love you. Thank you to the incredible BookLeaf publishing team for providing me the time, flexibility, ownership, and opportunity to do what I love: share stories. And thank you most of all to Kenzie and Aidan— for seeing me through every single deadline, every breakdown, every spell of writer's block. Thank you Kenzie for reading and re-reading every poem 1,001 times. Thank you Aidan for editing my ramblings without hesitation, for making them beautiful. This collection belongs to you both as much as I, and I can never articulate how grateful I am to have the two of you in my life. Thank you for hearing my scribbles that evening in March and telling me they were something different, something important.

PREFACE

there is a beautiful mess inherent in life, a gray area

that exists in the overlap between "was" and "is" an

"will be."

what will be

?

!

.

for kenzie and aidan

you make me a better version of myself— a

better me than mine

epiphany

/əˈpifənē/

a moment of sudden revelation or insight 4

ETHER

look up.

the mind cannot eclipse what she does not perceive. the moon

knows the sun well,

and thus harbors the strength to silence her. what

goes on in the ether—

a rearrangement of fates,

a blithe, meaningless construction?

can atmospheric bliss give rise to any

act of creation?

or are we responsible for the burden

of our own peace,

in our own void

down below?

EROS

what is wind if not a forgery of a kiss?

a fine calligrapher,

a worthy impersonator of your touch.

the separation of

predetermined eloquence

from

unprecedented passion—

willows sway in the breeze, emboldened by wisps of

yesterday.

like wind, i wonder where your touch came from. it seems

eternal, omniscient:

an amalgamation of history delineated in texts i've yet to

peruse.

but that smell of old ink and your perfume, and

sage and rose

persists even so.

(the eclipse of rarity and oddity)

you come from everywhere, from nowhere, my

favorite visitor

CRAYONS

sometimes i think beautiful thoughts

and i promise them that they'll last.

i swear that i'll retain them,

that they won't fall flat from my psyche to the

pavement below,

nestling permanently

into the cracks of the earth

after a day,

an hour,

a moment.

but i lie to them.

i lie to myself.

for the world brims with beauty—

each new fragment of laughter,

each new touching phrase,

each new sliver of inspiration

gently and brilliantly eclipses the last.

my life engulfs me in a warm sea of words,

swirling tendrils of language.

wanting to capture everything,

finding myself at a loss for words,

of words.

untethered by pen and paper

i leave them behind,

like so many unfinished drawings on a child's desk,

surrounded by crayons.

how lovely, to be eluded by my own mind, my
own joy.
i laugh.

my crayons are melting in the sun.

MIDPOINT

i am secure

tunnel walls smear by through

the lens of a subway window

to my right.

my foot rests on the edge of a lip in the wall. you in

front of me

you to my left

the two of you

all around me,

engulfing me.

i have never felt so at ease

in a rush

—

fuck.

the subway stopped.

bliss momentarily disrupted; we might be late— quick,

patch the puncture in our tranquility before triviality can

re-deflate our existence. we are, after all, on borrowed

time.

perhaps it's serendipitous.

maybe we can just stay here forever.

perpetual calm.

and we're moving again.

i saw graffiti on the wall

"one..." something

one what?

i thought i saw a k.

my mind completes the rest:

i hope it said kiss.

we scurry along like so many rats through tunnels we built

and decided to name

the 1

the R

the W

uptown, downtown

one of you is ardently scribbling away,

writing your novel, building a world i cannot see but will

surely become privy to by this time tomorrow.

ink scratches against paper as the dim, sallow light of the D

line glances across your skin.

one of you is simply existing beside me. i say simply; you and

i both know the task is anything but.

we breathe—

a gentle transfer of peace occurs between us as we notice each other.

being.

we tense in succession as the car fills to the brim; people with

places to go, people to see.

people.

secretly, serenely human.

stand clear of the closing doors, please.

ROSÉ

don't move,

i whisper to myself.

don't make a sound.

hold your breath.

encase this perfect moment within your lungs, contain

it—

shackle it to your ribs,

embalm it with your blood and

seal it with every fiber of your being,

so that even in death it will appear

fresh, vibrant,

immortalized with painful specificity,

recalled in milliseconds.

internalize it,

instill it.

i want to bottle this like fine wine.

harvesting

extracting every detail from the present, each

facet within my frame of focus—

the way your hair falls on either side of your face, caressing

your cheeks.

what i wouldn't give to trade places with your

tresses.

the scent of fresh grasses, bent and broken beneath our

blankets,

relinquishing their essence to the surrounding air with

nary a sigh.

the precise color of your sweater (mental paint swatches

are lain against the fabric in a vain attempt to match the

shade).

and how the silence is broken only by the wind, or by the

lilt of your voice—

truthfully, i can barely tell the difference.

pressing

innumerable specifics are sorted and crushed,

compressed into a pint-sized snapshot

of the now.

the life in the moment fades as i begin to extract every

ounce of what is cosmic, fathomless about this.

joy and laughter,

peace and calm

the taste of love rekindled

runs in rivulets across the surface of my mind, dripping

between each gyri and into the sulci, pervading every

groove of my brain

with brilliant incalculability.

the instant of true creation.

over days,

weeks,

years,

the image will warp,

the potent must of a pure, unfettered vision meets

with the agent of change,

the yeast of time and opinion and wishful thinking. the edges

of my image soften, your smile smears slightly

as my psyche coalesces fluid and igniting agent to produce

mental ethanol:

the intoxication of here, of now.

later, we tend to call it nostalgia.

clarification

dust, skin, marc is removed as i scrape

the bottom of the barrel,

soaking up every last drop of today.

i strain out the settled filaments that

do not serve me,

aiming to sift the worry from the calm, the anxiety about

walking back in the dark from the tranquility of the

sunset,

whose hues are only overshadowed by the

kaleidoscopic, shimmering tone of your eyes.

but i cannot extract every bit of dust, every crumb of

imperfection.

beauty in comparative sadness— it is what makes this

particular year so very special.

the notes of incompletion.

aging

the instance is bottled and corked,

continually infused with the tannins of time and

recollection;

my hippocampus serves as its oaky chamber. the longer it

sits, the richer and softer the flavors. but the last remaining

enzymes demand a fair exchange for their labor.

"time heals all wounds—"

i've never truly believed that.

but it certainly blurs all memories.

a few droplets of a meticulously-captured moment

evaporate into the air beyond the barrel-slats and are lost.

the precise texture of your blanket,

the subspecies of flower i tucked behind your ear, the exact

timbre of your mirth—

did you laugh in

B ♭ or C?

how bittersweet that there are always some vapors lost to

the passage of time.

the angels' share, winemakers call it.

but i am happy to share you with the angels. i owe

them, after all—

they shared you with me.

CONTRACT

don't get comfortable.

you're not staying long.

i've invited you here to listen,

not to speak.

i think you're done;

enough out of you for a lifetime.

incredible.

your precision, your resonance.

twenty-four hours would be more than sufficient for your

task.

twenty-four words.

and you

had

years.

you will never be more than mine,

bite your tongue.

how does it feel

to taste the control you

so genially serve to others?

hors d'oeuvres that smack

of power plays,

a main course of dereliction,

paired with wine, of course—

there are notes of your own fragility,

a symphonic bouquet of entitlement,

the same narcissistic drivel,

scribbled in different fonts.

it's been a long time since i had a homecooked meal.

so sit there and listen.

listen to me.

i want you to hear a single word spoken in the

exact timbre and lilt

of the voice you tried

so desperately to stifle.

my hair

my neck

my body

my voice

my life

not yours, not ever.

mine.

PEN

i long for words, i thirst for words—

their fragrant scent pervades the air,

through which fly birds

whose nests are built of nouns and verbs and hair.

between the bark of every tree,

in cracks of mossy silk,

run gushing streams of poetry—

they flow like honeyed milk.

the worlds we build are golden,

divinely picturesque,

but never quite emboldened

'til we free them from the desk.

when i die you have to promise

that you'll dip me into ink,

and finally with one last kiss,

into the words i'll sink.

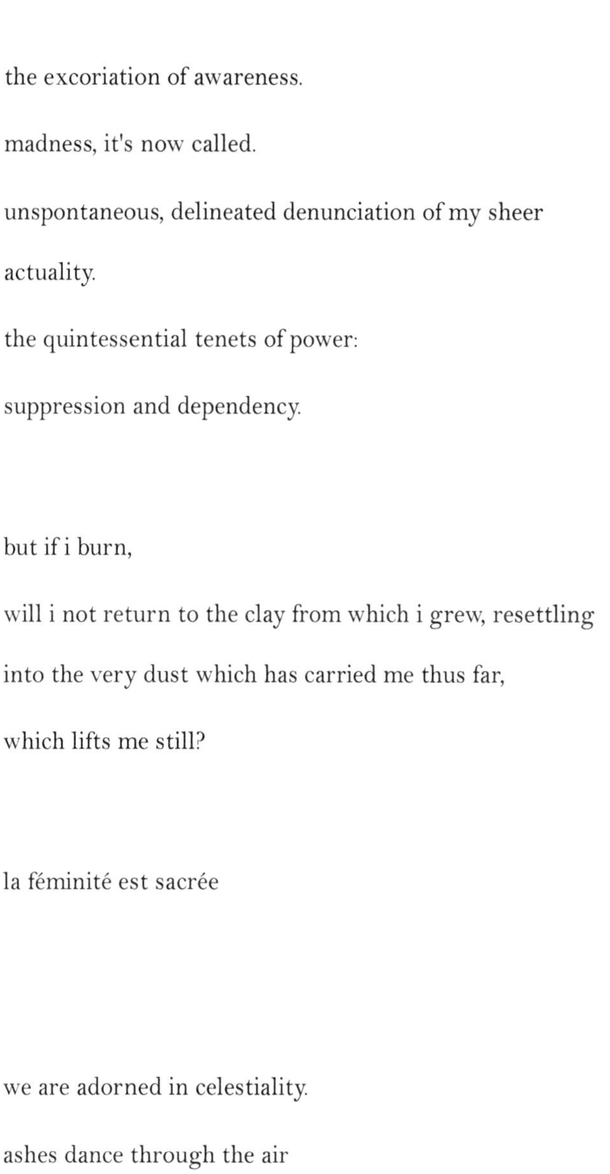

ESSE

the excoriation of awareness.

madness, it's now called.

unspontaneous, delineated denunciation of my sheer

actuality.

the quintessential tenets of power:

suppression and dependency.

but if i burn,

will i not return to the clay from which i grew, resettling

into the very dust which has carried me thus far,

which lifts me still?

la féminité est sacrée

we are adorned in celestiality.

ashes dance through the air

and land gently in the tresses you aimed to shackle. aimed to.

for still, air allowing, i flicker.

and still, pen to page, i persist.

i have ink on my fingers

words stain fingers.

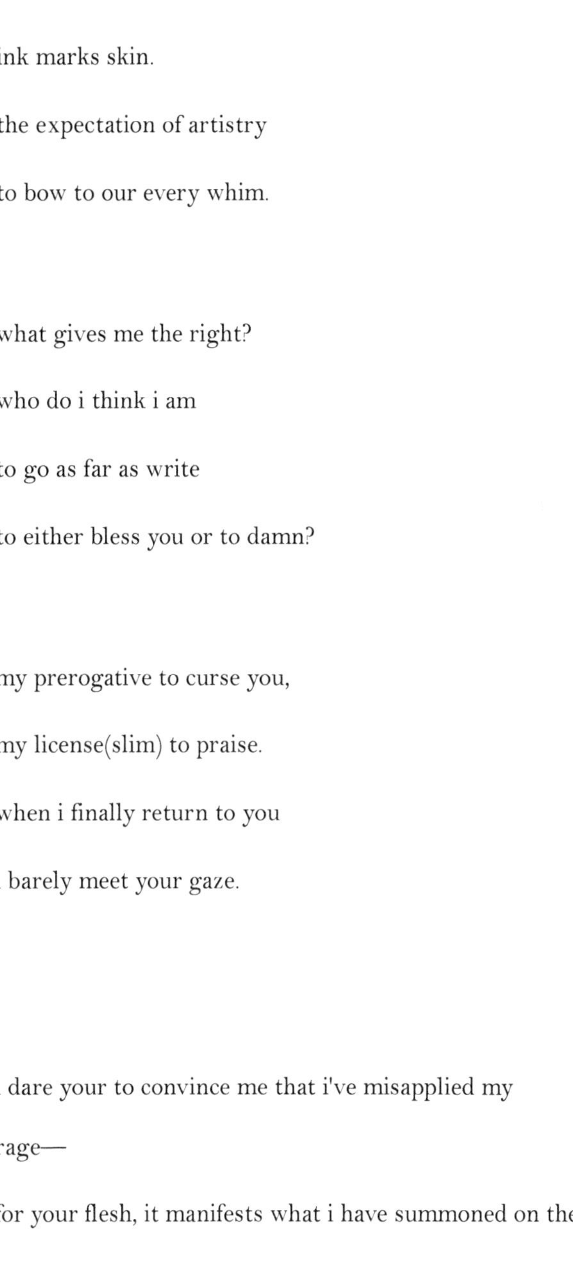

ink marks skin.

the expectation of artistry

to bow to our every whim.

what gives me the right?

who do i think i am

to go as far as write

to either bless you or to damn?

my prerogative to curse you,

my license(slim) to praise.

when i finally return to you

i barely meet your gaze.

i dare your to convince me that i've misapplied my

rage—

for your flesh, it manifests what i have summoned on the

page.

K

you are light and breath

and sound and wind and love,

and every single speck of peace that

wedges itself between moments of chaos bears

your name.

i find you in the moments when

i smile for no discernible reason,

when i spot a daffodil on my walk,

when i smell powdered sugar and french vanilla.

you move through the world,

compassion personified—

lamps click on when you enter a room,

a flood of luminescence.

you are sunshine on a hardwood floor.

you are fresh tulips and patterned dishtowels; you are

tight hugs, stained glass, and

a knowing glance— oh! and i forgot to tell you i know

what beauty is now.

you squeeze my hand, and there it is:

the feeling of wishing i could keep a straight face, of

knowing i am safe, of hearing windchimes.

& breeze and song

characterize your laugh, your smile,

the way your fingers tap and the way

you play with your hair when

nobody is looking.

a

i can't believe that i actually wheeze when you

make me laugh.

i love the way your mind works.

i love the way you think,

the meticulously spontaneous

manner in which you write.

i love how you use words to describe feelings that i

am never even able to name—

you give them families, pasts, dreams, secrets.

the scent of pines and of

burnt coffee follows you down the stairs and lingers

when you leave a room.

I'M HERE

your forehead furrows as

your eyebrows meet

to discuss, to touch base, to analyze

and to find the perfect word

for orange or warm

or happy or

miracle.

you ask me and i reply:

amber, emberous,

euphoric,

a day with you in my life.

CATCHBREATH

my thoughts come in gasps,

rising through murky webs i crafted for myself— or did i

inherit them?

i guess we'll never know

if i scrawl them down fast enough

i can catch them,

ribbons of ash floating down

from the sky

will i be able to grasp them

or will they be tumbled away by the sheer

movement of the air as i

attempt to entrap them,

the sheer exertion of my effort,

my entitlement, gusting them

just out of reach—

do i think they are mine to own?

a bold assumption.

ULTIMATUM

she had something to say.

did she forget, or was she stifled

just long enough to dissipate

the lucidity of resistance verbate?

vague recollections drift through the sky,

settling into the turf.

something of freedom.

the stakes for recall never higher,

scraping the heavens with their necessity. life or

death,

love or loneliness.

which is more dire?

for to die is to be at peace,

but to find oneself loveless is to

serve a sentence of

perpetual incompletion.

but i yield my time to the silence—

she still has something to say.

wait.

BASEMENT

have you ever wondered what it's like

to watch two people fall into love?

headfirst, into the deep end?

the wondering, the eyeless clasp of hands as ten fingers

subtly greet one another without word or thought.

how far-fetched to find two tones

comprised within the same harmonic scale, two

beams of light of identical wavelength.

what is love— how do those outside the equation explain

what two souls enthralled cannot even articulate?

i will do my best.

it seems to me that it can only be defined in

flashes—

old-fashioned camera bulbs shatter onto the ground

below

and crunch under now-lighter feet.

the gazes that occur between whole-body laughter, the

almost-kisses as faces move closer than anticipated,

as skin brushes against skin.

and the smiles that the other one never sees but that

remind me of how much radiance still pervades that mess

we call the human experience.

[UNTITLED]

you ask me what i need—

i need a reason.

a reason to write,

and not just for writing's sake.

creation for the sole purpose of creation is at

best self-serving

and at worst cyclical.

and cycles have never done

anyone any good—

history repeats itself.

art repeats itself.

i repeat my goddamn self

over and over and over

and over and over

and over and

over.

trapped, pinned in an undertow

my own thoughts the continuous, deafening rush of

the river

as i drown slowly in my own mind.

[UNTITLED II]

i feel like i may need to

derail my consciousness.

just turn it off and back on again,

toggle the switch.

complete reset

try it again

is it working now

lift

my roots are growing out.

color bleeds—

no, doesn't even bleed.

color snaps into place and

jolts me back to reality,

each lock released from its follicle

is dual-toned, half jewel-toned.

brown meets lavender,

base overcomes whimsy,

pursuing it down the strand

with ardent menace.

why am i determined to

overtake what i create?

there is immediacy in the regression,

unprecedented speed in the return to truth. i cannot hide
forever.

my roots are growing out.

expensive, stubborn proof that i am still moving. 45

PRESSURIZED

lips dilute thoughts.

intentions are sifted through the fine mesh that

lives in the backs of our throats.

clay from silt,

truth eclipsed by cordiality

convention

fear

wants are saturated in subtext.

in innuendo.

we stumble through a fog of hints

we're done is softened

I NEED A BREAK

i don't want to take responsibility

i'm sorry you interpreted it that way

and i love you—

no words

just laughter, eye contact,

and a moment of silence broken by an

anyway

PERENNIAL

every year the poppies bloom.

the hills, browned from months of frost are

suddenly draped in tangerine,

gently cloaked in blossoms.

it happens almost overnight.

every year i can recall

with shame or nostalgia

or guilt

the version of me who

gazed upon the petaled ridges

only one rotation ago.

i can barely recognize her.

buds emerge from hibernating stems,

fronds of lace stretch to touch the sun,

to caress the breeze.

i raise my arms to do the same.

as i glance down,

the poppies and i celebrate the fact

that we are here another year,

that we have survived another winter.

as i stand on the hill,

we acknowledge one another—

we watch the sun rise together

and the scent of chilled dew

dances across the tip of my nose

i am still here.

RAIN

what.

i'm frustrated.

no— don't ask, don't.

that's even more infuriating

...

i can't figure out how to

describe the sound of the rain.

it's a gush, it's a roar, sure.

but it's more pervasive—

continuous, like the buzzing static of an

unclaimed am/fm station.

WHERE'S THE WORD?

how could any language adequately articulate the

incessant patter of an impending river? it sounds like

potential:

destruction or creation

creation *and* destruction.

the emergence of spring,

the budding bloom of the lupine—

its purple pips lean into the drizzle.

and the gurgling, rushing possibility

of splintered puddles,

impromptu mirrors shattered by

tires on the highway.

deluge, maybe.

[UNTITLED III]

embers in my chest

tingle across my thighs

beads of sweat brim just

under the surface of each pore,

barely shy of spilling out

onto the skin of my neck.

barely.

what spill instead are words—

physical nausea results in

lingual upheaval

as i am repeatedly compressed and released under

hydraulics.

the butterflies in my stomach

feel more like vultures now,

or a murder of crows.

their wings smash against the confines of my

abdomen.

those pangs must be their pecks

as loving you eats me

slowly from the inside out.

CONIFEROUS

what would you find if you cut me open? if you

bisected me— torso from pelvis,

sliced me straight across?

sinew and muscle and fat and bone and blood,

yes.

logically, i know that's what's inside.

i can touch my chest and find the

slightly pliable, barred shelves of my ribs; i can feel

my organs digging into the waist of my favorite

jeans.

but how do i know that if you snipped me apart with a

mammoth pair of shears

that i wouldn't simply be

filled with cotton,

or candies, like a children's piñata?

who's to say that if you

cut me open and looked down,

you wouldn't find the established rings of a tree,

delineating the stages of my life in sweet,

pine-scented layers?

FLY

i shut the window with a thud and

turn the latch.

the cries of horns honking and

the yawns of a metropolis awakening

muffle with immediacy.

it is raining today.

the cool scent of mist colliding

with yesterday's sun-drenched pavement is

wafting into the air,

reaching me even at the highest story,

where i perch like a goldfinch on my

borrowed windowsill.

my bliss has yet to be sedated by

disenchantment—

i wonder if one day the un-dream will begin to gush

gently across my soul,

permeating my joy

like the rain dribbling into the sidewalk cracks

below.

not yet. please, not yet.

2:35 A.M.

i'm up late again

you're not here this time

but that's impossible—

you exist with me in perpetuity.

i think

i think i have this compulsive need

to be at least mildly unhappy

all of the time.

then i can juxtapose calm and chaos,

can have some gripping point,

some safety railing to

keep me from tumbling down the stairs into

unreality.

laughter can't exist without silence,

that sort of thing.

i worry that i've only earned

so much time to be happy.

it's not cynical.

it's calculating

to dilute emotion,

because what if i squander,

what if i use up my share of goodness

too quickly?

and so i ration,

i microdose experience.

i should go to sleep

but you've shown up again.

do i stay with you or

save us for tomorrow,

if tomorrow ever comes?

TRIPLE-WORD SCORE

this is pointless.

what am i saying—

i'm rambling, overturning

a bag of lexiconical nonsense

onto a metaphysical table

(thought is just a high-stakes game of Scrabble) and still

cramming words blatantly

into spaces they never earned, i never earned. who is it

for?

irrational, isn't it.

she's afraid of scrawling just to feel something, just to

prove to herself that her musings are anything but

arbitrary.

cacophony

who's up there?

who's writing?

whose words will delineate today?

i am a multitude,

splinters of my ethos

squabble over the pen.

anxiety-induced overlap,

we're losing it—

time, words, coherence.

can we talk about this rationally?

this isn't some sort of psycho

physical socratic seminar

you don't choose us,

we are merely here

    here-ly

good one

focus.

what was that?

        i miss them

slow down.

                                you know what i was thinking?

                                    thought is witchcraft…

                                  neuronal necromancy—

everyone SHUT UP!

i can't think.

but without you i can't think. fuck.

each shard of my psyche is

a precocious attention whore—

pick me

pick me

PICK ME.

—but you are me.

so where does that leave us?

if you are me, then who am i?

...

someone write it down.

PERSPECTIVE

in our apartment.

body sprawled on a bed which

barely fits the room,

head protruding from the window.

i rest gently on the ledge

as my mind points northwest

through the bars of the fire escape.

i gaze up at the sky;

it drizzles, and i see the world

in the upside-down.

the raindrops are only visible against the peeling

black railing—

they come in flashes, in droves, directionless. 65

are they still falling downwards,

or did they change trajectory

as i settled onto the sill, when i wasn't looking? what if

gravity is just temporarily out of order— *we apologize for*

the inconvenience

i hear dishes clink and

the trickle of the creek in Central Park and the

sound of your voice mingles with Fleetwood Mac

as the clouds drip gently onto my cheeks and my

lips and my hair

and i cannot tell if it is the rain or

my own tears filling my eyes.

then i remember that i am wearing glasses. 66

gardenia

belligerent nostalgia.

your skin in the moonlight,

the smell of your soap—

it lingers in the most unexpected places.

i'll find a cloud of you in that

corner of my room that i venture into the least, where i

keep my broom and

my laundry basket and

the box i never open.

i'll step on a shard of you, a pebble,

on a crowded city street as i pass by a jasmine tree on the

fifteenth day in April—

spring lives here, and so do you.

you are everywhere, you are constant,

like gravity or sunsets or

my student debt.

and i am dwindling to nothing,

like water disappearing into the basil's potting soil, like the

ice cube in my glass becoming the condensation that glazes

my fingers,

like time.

you follow me down the road

and into the trees, you stop me

and the last remnants of your kiss have escaped their box

somehow

they hold me as i cry.

rock show

i taste raindrops.

they fall into my nostrils,

pool in my eye sockets,

run between the creases in my forehead and chin and fill

every pore

with the tears of some cloud.

as i dance, there is music somewhere

and i am bobbing amongst the soundwaves,

enveloped by the ringing harmonies of the

whitecaps as they break against my chest

i am happy.

you are here.

the downpour on my skin and my skull sounds like

drumming—

my heart claps along

and i am imbued with a rhythm that

ripples all around me,

a syncopated existence

and i am twirling in the deluge(that *was* it) of the dreams i

thought i would have awoken from by now, drenched in

well i did

to your *you could never*

i stick out my tongue to catch the flavor of my life; it tastes

like Swedish fish and blonde roast and overripe raspberries.

the beat drops,

the drops beat,

and i am flying

into the velvet ceiling of an open sky.

i am happy.

i am here.

VENN

do you ever notice the colors

on the backs of your eyelids?

i only do in moments of stillness; after all, perception

is inherently dependent on breath.

sometimes i remember that they're there— dancing,

shifting, warping.

they exist only for themselves, i their

only audience.

sometimes i think their color changes based on the

lights in the room, or the sun—

hot, white, yellow, bright.

but sometimes i think maybe they are

handcrafted for me:

magenta chartreuse

periwinkle emerald

> gold *burnt orange:* coquelicot— *think tangerines*

> *and nostalgia.*

ironic that there's a name for that

specific shade of orange and not for

the current state of my soul.

and purple.

i'm partial to lavender, but more often than not it's

royal— royalty in shapes i can't

pronounce or name.

plum hues engulf my existence:

blue and red converge to form

amaranthine, mauve, lilac.

maybe i'll just use colors to name what i cannot— my

dreams are drenched in mulberry,

my heart stained with Bordeaux.

my love is tinted in falu—

think ruby, but deeper, darker, more pervasive, toned

with brown and navy.

almost a new shade of purple.

maybe i can just conjure a new word

for the color i see when i close my eyelids and think of

you.

prâmdremes

(from the French— *take my soul*)